A country calendar of RURAL RHYMES

poems chosen by Robin Holmes

Wood engravings by Reynolds Stone

EYRE METHUEN

First published 1980
by Eyre Methuen Ltd
11 New Fetter Lane, London EC4P 4EE
Copyright © 1980 Robin Holmes
Wood engravings © 1980 Janet Stone

Produced by Rock Lambert
17 Albemarle Street, London W1X 4AA
Filmset by Rowland Phototypesetting Ltd
Bury St Edmunds, Suffolk
Printed in Great Britain by
St Edmundsbury Press
Bury St Edmunds

For Marj

British Library Cataloguing in Publication Data
A country calendar of rural rhymes
1 Pastoral poetry, English
2 Country life – Great Britain – Poetry
I Holmes, Robin   II Stone, Reynolds
821'.008'032   PR1195.P3

ISBN 0-413-47540-9

INTRODUCTION

In 1974 an abbreviated version of John Clare's *Shepherd's Calendar* was allotted five minutes' broadcasting time at five to nine in the morning on the first day of each month on BBC Radio Three. The sight and scents of the countryside Clare's poems evoked paved the way for a wider selection of seasonal verse, broadcast as 'Rural Rhymes' during 1978 and 1979.

Two successive controllers of Radio Three – Stephen Hearst and Ian McIntyre – thought it might appeal to listeners, even at that early and unkindly time of day. They were right and my thanks go to them. The broadcasts were planned to show, season by season, the appearance and the moods of the British countryside. Each month contained poems by several different authors, sometimes linked in feeling, sometimes sharply contrasted. The names of the poets were not announced until the end of the programme, which made listening a gentle guessing game. I hope that readers too may be led on, poem by poem, through each month.

John Clare still earns most space in the book. He appears at least once in almost every month; but then the discovery in a rented house, at a bleak period of the war, of J W Tibble's two-volume edition of *The Poems of John Clare* was one of the most significant events of my life. Of the other poets, it has been argued that some few of them turn up month by month too regularly. I can only answer that they are favourites of mine. All were countrymen; many combine the impartiality of a naturalist's eye with the transforming passion of a poet's.

There are a lot of poems about birds. I love them too.

CONTENTS

JANUARY

FEBRUARY

MARCH

APRIL

MAY

JUNE

JULY

AUGUST

6

JANUARY

The Old Year's gone away
  To nothingness and night:
We cannot find him all the day
  Nor hear him in the night:
He left no footstep, mark, or place
  In either shade or sun:
The last year he'd a neighbour's face,
  In this he's known by none.

All nothing everywhere:
  Mists we on mornings see
Have more of substance when they're here
  And more of form than he.
He was a friend by every fire,
  In every cot and hall –
A guest to every heart's desire,
  And now he's naught at all.

Old papers thrown away,
  Old garments cast aside,
The talk of yesterday,
  Are things identified;
But time once torn away
  No voices can recall:
The eve of New Year's Day
  Left the Old Year lost to all.   *John Clare*

7

He was the one man I met up in the woods
That stormy New Year's morning; and at first sight,
Fifty yards off, I could not tell how much
Of that strange tripod was a man. His body
Bowed horizontal, was supported equally
By legs at one end, by a rake at the other:
Thus he rested, far less like a man than
His wheel-barrow in profile was like a pig.
But when I saw it was an old man bent,
At the same moment came into my mind
The games at which boys bend thus, *High-cocolorum*,
Or *Fly-the-garter*, and *Leap-frog*. At the sound
Of footsteps he began to straighten himself;
His head rolled under his cape like a tortoise's;
He took an unlit pipe out of his mouth
Politely ere I wished him 'A Happy New Year',
And with his head cast upward sideways muttered-
So far as I could hear through the trees' roar –
'Happy New Year, and may it come fastish, too',
While I strode by and he turned to raking leaves.

Edward Thomas

They said, It will be like snow falling –
To-night a hollow wind beating the laurels,
And in the morning quiet, the laurels quiet,
The soft sky resting on the treetops and
The earth not crying any more.

I read it would be safe, like snow lying
Locked in a secret promise with the ground.
And the clear distances, the friendly hills
Would whisper, It is easy, easy as sleep
To the lost traveller frozen in the field.

But now it's come, how different without
Those reassuring voices. Now I face
The bright white glare of January, naked
Among the clashing laurels, while the earth
Stumbles and cries like any lonely lover.

Sidney Keyes

From nuddling night's embrace now chill
　　The winter's waxing days begin,
Dull reddening o'er the east's blea hill
　　And creeping sad and shyly in!
Now gilds the sun each bare tree-top
　　And pale peeps thro' each window light,
While from the eaves the ickles drop,
　　That eke afresh their tails at night.

The snows and rime lodge everywhere;
　　Each cot in dazzling white is drest;
Nor thatch nor wither'd weeds appear
　　Where birds their numbing feet may rest.
And every twig thro' wood and plain
　　Where summer hung her greening bough,
Wild winter's mockery clothes again
　　With hoary shapes and shadows now.

John Clare

We listened to your birds to-night
By the firelight,
The nightingales that trilled to us
From moonlit boughs.

Though golden snow-flakes from the gloom
Looked in the room,
Those birds' clear voices lingered on
Your gramophone.

'Good-night' we said and as I go
High-heeled with snow
I almost hope to hear one now
From a bare bough.　　　*Andrew Young*

Briefly, the Long-tailed tit
May be distinguished from the Short-tailed tit
In that its tail is long.
Think of it that way and you can't go wrong.

We may with equal certainty
Identify the hen
Blackcap, she being capped with red; and again,
The cock-bird who, concealed,
Is self-revealed by his distinctive song –
Unless he churrs
In imitation of the Garden-warbler,
Which frequently occurs.

Or take the Long-eared owl,
Different, by reason of its prominent 'ears'
From that other delightful fowl
The Short-eared owl,
Though both, in fact, have none.

This ornithologist idea of fun
Brings one to tears,
So give thanks for the Wagtail family,
Whose identification, they say,
Is child's play:

For the (migrant) White wagtail's back
Is grey,
Unlike the (resident) Pied wagtail's,
Which is black
(But fades with the first snowfalls of the year
To a pale grey, they fear).
Then there's the Grey wagtail, though
This obliging fellow
Requires no explanation,
Being – as you will know –
Bright yellow.   *Betty Parvin*

FEBRUARY

Where does comfort's bosom glow?
Where lives he a tenant now?
In snug places out of doors,
Fields, or woods, or rushy moors?
No, for winter occupies
Every bit of earth and skies;
Overhead the clouds are dull,
Underfoot the roads are full
Of mire and sludge, and water too,
That slushes in the ploughman's shoe,
And spatters from the hasty horse,
That has the meadow's floods to cross.
So where is comfort? can it be,
Underneath the woodland tree,
Where the shepherd still about
Found primrose buds ere March was out,
And maidens in the summer lay
On their elbows in the hay?
And labour's self, that could not bear
To wear his lazy jacket there,
Complains as much as any one
And puts another garment on;
And still, do all he ever may,
He cannot keep the cold away.
He buttons up as on he goes,
His hat he slouches o'er his nose,
And, glad to keep the storm behind,
He turns his back upon the wind,
And knocks his hands, and stamps his toes,
And in his pockets as he goes

11

Will hide them – yet, do what he may,
He can't get out of winter's way.
Where is comfort? maybe, here;
Sitting in the elbow chair,
With a pipe beneath his nose,
While the smoke at leisure goes
Up agen the mantel-tree
In a wreath of silver-grey;
With a jug of gingered ale,
Or little book that owns a tale
For merry-making, not too long,
And what is better, shorter song –
While in the chimney-top the snow
Falls right upon the fire below
With just a little quench, and then
It seems to burn as bright agen.   *John Clare*

The keener tempests come; and, fuming dun,
From all the livid east, or piercing north,
Thick clouds ascend; in whose capacious womb
A vapoury deluge lies, to snow congealed.
Heavy they roll their fleecy world along,
And the sky saddens with the gathered storm.
Through the hushed air the whitening shower
        descends,
At first thin-wavering; till at last the flakes
Fall broad, and wide, and fast, dimming the day
With a continual flow. The cherished fields
Put on their winter robe of purest white.
'Tis brightness all, save where the new snow melts
Along the mazy current. Low, the woods
Bow their hoar head; and, ere the languid sun,
Faint from the west, emits his evening ray,
Earth's universal face, deep-hid and chill,
Is one wild dazzling waste, that buries wide
The works of man. Drooping, the labourer-ox
Stands covered o'er with snow, and then demands

The fruit of all his toil. The fowls of heaven,
Tamed by the cruel season, crowd around
The winnowing store, and claim the little boon
Which providence assigns them. One alone,
The redbreast, sacred to the household gods,
Wisely regardful of the embroiling sky,
In joyless fields and thorny thickets leaves
His shivering mates, and pays to trusted man
His annual visit. Half-afraid, he first
Against the window beats; then brisk alights
On the warm hearth; then, hopping o'er the floor,
Eyes all the smiling family askance,
And pecks, and starts, and wonders where he is;
Till, more familiar grown, the table-crumbs
Attract his slender feet. . . .   *James Thomson*

The snows of February had buried Christmas
Deep in the woods, where grew self-seeded
The fir-trees of a Christmas yet unknown,
Without a candle or a strand of tinsel.

Nevertheless when, hand in hand, plodding
Between the frozen ruts, we lovers paused
And 'Christmas trees!' cried suddenly together,
Christmas was there again, as in December.

We velveted our love with fantasy
Down a long vista-row of Christmas trees,
Whose coloured candles slowly guttered down
As grandchildren came trooping round our knees.

But he knew better, did the Christmas robin –
The murderous robin with his breast aglow
And legs apart, in a spade-handle perched:
He prophesied more snow, and worse than snow.
                                        Robert Graves

The summer nests uncovered by autumn wind,
Some torn, others dislodged, all dark,
Everyone sees them: low or high in tree,
Or hedge, or single bush, they hang like a mark.

Since there's no need of eyes to see them with
I cannot help a little shame
That I missed most, even at eye's level, till
The leaves blew off and made the seeing no game.

'Tis a light pang. I like to see the nests
Still in their places, now first known,
At home and by far roads. Boys knew them not,
Whatever jays and squirrels may have done.

And most I like the winter nests deep-hid
That leaves and berries fell into:
Once a dormouse dined there on hazel-nuts,
And grass and goose-grass seeds found soil
     and grew.   *Edward Thomas*

I leant upon a coppice gate
  When Frost was spectre-gray,
And Winter's dregs made desolate
  The weakening eye of day.
The tangled bine-stems scored the sky
  Like strings of broken lyres,
And all mankind that haunted nigh
  Had sought their household fires.

The land's sharp features seemed to be
  The Century's corpse outleant,
His crypt the cloudy canopy,
  The wind his death-lament.
The ancient pulse of germ and birth
  Was shrunken hard and dry,
And every spirit upon earth
  Seemed fervourless as I.

At once a voice arose among
  The bleak twigs overhead
In a full-hearted evensong
  Of joy illimited;
An aged thrush, frail, gaunt, and small,
  In blast-beruffled plume,
Had chosen thus to fling his soul
  Upon the growing gloom.

So little cause for carolings
  Of such ecstatic sound
Was written on terrestrial things
  Afar or nigh around,
That I could think there trembled through
  His happy good-night air
Some blessed Hope, whereof he knew
  And I was unaware.   *Thomas Hardy*

Frost called to water 'Halt!'
And crusted the moist snow with sparkling salt;
Brooks, their own bridges, stop,
And icicles in long stalactites drop,
And tench in water-holes
Lurk under gluey glass like fish in bowls.

In the hard-rutted lane
At every footstep breaks a brittle pane,
And tinkling trees ice-bound,
Changed into weeping willows, sweep the ground;
Dead boughs take root in ponds
And ferns on windows shoot their ghostly fronds.

But vainly the fierce frost
Interns poor fish, ranks trees in an armed host,
Hangs daggers from house-eaves
And on the windows ferny ambush weaves;
In the long war grown warmer
The sun will strike him dead and strip his armour.
                                   Andrew Young

MARCH

March, month of 'many weathers', wildly comes
In hail, and snow, and rain, and threatening hums,
And floods; while often at his cottage-door
The shepherd stands, to hear the distant roar
Loosed from the rushing mills and river-locks,
With thundering sound and overpowering shocks.
From bank to bank, along the meadow lea,
The river spreads, and shines a little sea;
While, in the pale sunlight, a watery brood
Of swopping white birds flock about the flood.

  Yet Winter seems half weary of his toil;
And round the ploughmen, on the elting soil,
Will thread a minute's sunshine wild and warm,
Through the ragg'd places of the swimming storm;
And oft the shepherd in his path will spy
The little daisy in the wet grass lie,
That to the peeping sun uncloses gay,
Like Labour smiling on a holiday;
And where the steep bank fronts the southern sky,
By lanes or brooks where sunbeams love to lie,
A cowslip-peep will open faintly coy,
Soon seen and gather'd by a wondering boy . . .

16

. . . Muffled in baffles, leather coat and gloves,
The hedger toils, oft scaring rustling doves
From out the hedgerows, who in hunger browze
The chocolate berries on the ivy boughs,
Or flocking fieldfares, speckled like the thrush,
Picking the red haw from the sweeing bush,
That come and go on winter's chilling wing,
And seem to share no sympathy with spring.

John Clare

And see where surly Winter passes off
Far to the north, and calls his ruffian blasts.
His blasts obey, and quit the howling hill,
The shattered forest, and the ravaged vale;
While softer gales succeed, at whose kind touch,
Dissolving snows in livid torrents lost,
The mountains lift their green heads to the sky.
   As yet the trembling year is unconfirmed,
And Winter oft at eve resumes the breeze,
Chills the pale morn, and bids his driving sleets
Deform the day delightless; so that scarce
The bittern knows his time with bill engulfed
To shake the sounding marsh; or from the shore
The plovers when to scatter o'er the heath,
And sing their wild notes to the listening waste.

James Thomson

Now March's beech trees, rising dry
And clear, before the pale blue sky
Show fair, with rind all shining white
Along their limbs and through their height,
Ere yet their leaves have thicken'd green,
To make, above the ground, a screen
Against the flighty wind that strews
The whirling dead leaves round our shoes.
   Though March's silv'ry moon is cold
   The sun becomes of glowing gold.

Now grain, wherewith the sowers trust
The ground, upwakes through warmer dust
To summer life, as world-wide days
Warm opening buds on quiv'ring sprays,
And flocks of glossy rooks alight
On sunny ground in sinking flight,
Too often slain for theft of wheat,
When taking noisome worms for meat.
　　Though March's silv'ry moon is cold
　　The sun may soon be glowing gold.

William Barnes

Though buds still speak in hints
And frozen ground has set the flints
As fast as precious stones
And birds perch on the boughs, silent as cones,

Suddenly waked from sloth
Young trees put on a ten year's growth
And stones double their size,
Drawn nearer through field-glasses' greater eyes.

Why I borrow their sight
Is not to give small birds a fright
Creeping up close by inches;
I make the trees come, bringing tits and finches.

I lift a field itself
As lightly as I might a shelf,
And the rooks do not rage
Caught for a moment in my crystal cage.

And while I stand and look,
Their private lives an open book,
I feel so privileged
My shoulders prick, as though they were
　　half-fledged.　　　　　*Andrew Young*

They rose up in a twinkling cloud
And wheeled about and bowed
To settle on the trees
Perching like small clay images.

Then with a noise of sudden rain
They clattered off again
And over Ballard Down
They circled like a flying town.

Though one could sooner blast a rock
Than scatter that dense flock
That through the winter weather
Some iron rule has held together,

Yet in another month from now
Love like a spark will blow
Those birds the country over
To drop in trees, lover by lover.   *Andrew Young*

Over the land freckled with snow half-thawed
The speculating rooks at their nests cawed
And saw from elm-tops, delicate as flower of grass,
What we below could not see, Winter pass.

Edward Thomas

The groundflame of the crocus breaks
        the mould,
    Fair Spring slides hither o'er the
        Southern sea,
Wavers on her thin stem the snowdrop
        cold
    That trembles not to kisses of the bee:
Come, Spring, for now from all the
        dripping eaves
    The spear of ice has wept itself away,

And hour by hour unfolding woodbine
    leaves
  O'er his uncertain shadow droops the
    day.
She comes! The loosen'd rivulets run;
  The frost-bead melts upon her golden
    hair;
Her mantle, slowly greening in the Sun,
  Now wraps her close, now arching
    leaves her bare
  To breaths of balmier air;

Up leaps the lark, gone wild to welcome
    her,
  About her glance the tits, and shriek
    the jays,
Before her skims the jubilant woodpecker,
  The linnet's bosom blushes at her gaze,
While round her brows a woodland culver
    flits,
  Watching her large light eyes and
    gracious looks,
And in her open palm a halcyon sits
  Patient – the secret splendour of the
    brooks.
Come, Spring! She comes on waste and
    wood,
  On farm and field: but enter also here,
Diffuse thyself at will thro' all my blood,
  And, tho' thy violet sicken into sere,
  Lodge with me all the year!

                              Lord Tennyson

APRIL

Delightful weather for all sorts of moods!
And most for him grey morn and swarthy eve
Found rambling up the little narrow lane
Where primrose banks amid the hazelly woods
Peep most delightfully on passers-by;
While April's little clouds about the sky
Mottle and freak and unto fancy lie
Idling and ending travel for the day;
Till darker clouds sail up with cumbrous heave
South o'er the woods and scare them all away;
Then comes the rain, pelting with pearly drops
The primrose crowds until they stoop and lie
All fragrance to his mind that musing stops
Beneath the hawthorn till the shower is by.

John Clare

From the moist meadow to the withered hill,
Led by the breeze, the vivid verdure runs,
And swells, and deepens, to the cherished eye.
The hawthorn whitens; and the juicy groves
Put forth their buds, unfolding by degrees,
Till the whole leafy forest stands displayed,

In full luxuriance, to the sighing gales;
Where the deer rustle through the twining brake,
And the birds sing concealed. At once, arrayed
In all the colours of the flushing year
By nature's swift and secret-working hand,
The garden glows, and fills the liberal air
With lavish fragrance; while the promised fruit
Lies yet a little embryo, unperceived,
Within its crimson folds. Now from the town,
Buried in smoke and sleep, and noisome damps,
Oft let me wander o'er the dewy fields,
Where freshness breathes, and dash the trembling
    drops
From the bent bush, as through the verdant maze
Of sweet-briar hedges I pursue my walk.

James Thomson

When April scatters coins of primrose gold
Among the copper leaves in thickets old,
And singing skylarks from the meadows rise,
To twinkle like black stars in sunny skies;

When I can hear the small woodpecker ring
Time on a tree for all the birds that sing;
And hear the pleasant cuckoo, loud and long –
The simple bird that thinks two notes a song;

When I can hear the woodland brook, that could
Not drown a babe, with all his threatening mood;
Upon those banks the violets make their home,
And let a few small strawberry blossoms come:

When I go forth on such a pleasant day,
One breath outdoors takes all my care away;
It goes like heavy smoke, when flames take hold
Of wood that's green, and fill a grate with gold.

W H Davies

I watched a blackbird on a budding sycamore
One Easter Day when sap was stirring twigs
     to the core;
  I saw his tongue and crocus-coloured bill
  Parting and closing as he turned his trill;
  Then he flew down, seized on a stem of hay,
  And upped to where his building scheme was
     under way,
As if so sure a nest were never shaped on spray.

Thomas Hardy

Not the whole warbling grove in concert heard
When sunshine follows shower, the breast can thrill
Like the first summons, Cuckoo! of thy bill,
With its twin notes inseparably paired.
The captive 'mid damp vaults unsunned, unaired,
Measuring the periods of his lonely doom,
That cry can reach; and to the sick man's room
Sends gladness, by no languid smile declared.
The lordly eagle-race through hostile search
May perish; time may come when never more
The wilderness shall hear the lion roar;
But, long as cock shall crow from household perch
To rouse the dawn, soft gales shall speed thy wing,
And thy erratic voice be faithful to the Spring!

William Wordsworth

The thrushes sing as the sun is going,
     And the finches whistle in ones and pairs,
And as it gets dark loud nightingales
          In bushes
Pipe, as they can when April wears,
     As if all Time were theirs.

These are brand-new birds of twelve-months' growing,
Which a year ago, or less than twain,
No finches were, nor nightingales,
     Nor thrushes,
But only particles of grain,
    And earth, and air, and rain.   *Thomas Hardy*

I heard a thousand blended notes
While in a grove I sate reclined,
In that sweet mood when pleasant thoughts
Bring sad thoughts to the mind.

To her fair works did Nature link
The human soul that through me ran;
And much it grieved my heart to think
What man has made of man.

Through primrose tufts, in that green bower,
The periwinkle trailed its wreaths;
And 'tis my faith that every flower
Enjoys the air it breathes.

The birds around me hopped and played,
Their thought I cannot measure: –
But the least motion which they made,
It seemed a thrill of pleasure.

The budding twigs spread out their fan,
To catch the breezy air;
And I must think, do all I can,
That there was pleasure there.

If this belief from heaven be sent,
If such be Nature's holy plan,
Have I not reason to lament
What man has made of man?   *William Wordsworth*

MAY

Now the bright morning Star, Dayes harbinger,
Comes dancing from the East, and leads with her
The Flowry *May*, who from her green lap throws
The yellow Cowslip, and the pale Primrose.
  Hail bounteous *May* that dost inspire
  Mirth and youth, and warm desire,
  Woods and Groves, are of thy dressing,
  Hill and Dale, doth boast thy blessing.
Thus we salute thee with our early Song,
And welcom thee, and wish thee long.

John Milton

In suns and showers luxuriant May came forth
And spread her riches as of nothing worth,
Cowslips and daisies, buttercups, and crowds
Without a name as if they dropt from clouds,
On green and close and meadow everywhere,
So thick, the green did almost disappear
To gold and silver hues, and blooms did vie
With the rich grass' luxuriant mastery.

The simple shepherd in his early hour
With almost every footstep crushed a flower.
The winds did all they could, though oft in vain,
To raise and form them on their stalks again,
Yet some were crushed so much they could not rise,
Finding in poet's heart a room for sighs.
And those his dog beat down did hardly mind
But formed again as happy as the wind,
Leaving a lesson sad with every day
That harm falls most in man's destroying way:
And who could think in such a lovely time
And such a spot, where quiet seemed in prime,
As ne'er to be disturbed, that strife and fear
Like crouching tigers had howled havoc here?

John Clare

There was a roaring in the wind all night;
The rain came heavily and fell in floods;
But now the sun is rising calm and bright;
The birds are singing in the distant woods;
Over his own sweet voice the Stock-dove broods;
The Jay makes answer as the Magpie chatters;
And all the air is filled with pleasant noise of waters.

All things that love the sun are out of doors;
The sky rejoices in the morning's birth;
The grass is bright with rain-drops; – on the moors
The hare is running races in her mirth;
And with her feet she from the plashy earth
Raises a mist; that, glittering in the sun,
Runs with her all the way, wherever she doth run.

I was a Traveller then upon the moor;
I saw the hare that raced about with joy;
I heard the woods and distant waters roar;
Or heard them not, as happy as a boy:
The pleasant season did my heart employ:
My old remembrances went from me wholly;
And all the ways of men, so vain and melancholy.

But, as it sometimes chanceth, from the might
Of joy in minds that can no further go,
As high as we have mounted in delight
In our dejection do we sink as low;
To me that morning did it happen so;
And fears and fancies thick upon me came;
Dim sadness – and blind thoughts, I knew not,
        nor could name.   *William Wordsworth*

Let us go, then, exploring
This summer morning,
When all are adoring
The plum-blossom and the bee.
And humming and hawing
Let us ask of the starling
What he may think
On the brink
Of the dust-bin whence he picks
Among the sticks
Combings of scullion's hair.
What's life, we ask;
Life, Life, Life! cries the bird
As if he had heard . . .   *Virginia Woolf*

A thrush in the syringa sings.

'Hunger ruffles my wings, fear,
lust, familiar things.

Death thrusts hard. My sons
by hawk's beak, by stones,
trusting weak wings
by cat and weasel, die.

27

Thunder smothers the sky.
From a shaken bush I
list familiar things,
fear, hunger, lust.'

O gay thrush!   *Basil Bunting*

Sweet bird, that sing'st away the early hours,
Of winters past, or coming, void of care,
Well pleased with delights which present are,
Fair seasons, budding sprays, sweet-smelling
    flowers:
To rocks, to springs, to rills, from leafy bowers
Thou thy Creator's goodness dost declare,
And what dear gifts in thee he did not spare,
A stain to human sense in sin that lowers.
What soul can be so sick, which by thy songs
(Attir'd in sweetness) sweetly is not driven
Quite to forget Earth's turmoils, spites, and
    wrongs,
And lift a reverent eye and thought to Heaven?
Sweet, artless songster, thou my mind dost raise
To airs of spheres, yea, and to angels' lays.
                                    William Drummond

As o'er the hill with waving timber crown'd,
  In yonder drove, beneath an ash I lay;
  Where bloom'd the hawthorn with its
      snow-white may;
And gilt-cups brightly deck'd the grassy ground;

While merry hinds within the fields around,
  A-singing, ended some enliv'ning lay;
  I heard a waterfall, so far away
That stillness only brought its sullen sound;

And thought in silence, O thou peaceful place,
I would that summer weather could but last;
  And, in this northern land, the lovely face

Of nature could withstand the winter's blast;
  And I, from all my wordly cares set free,
  Could have, awhile, a happy home in thee.

William Barnes

In a between world, a world of amber,
The old cat on the sand-warm window-sill
Sleeps on the verge of nullity.

Spring sunshine has a quality
Transcending rooks and the hammering
Of those who hang new pictures,
Asking if it is worth it
To clamour and caw, to add stick to stick for ever.

If it is worth while really
To colonise any more the already populous
Tree of knowledge, to portion and reportion
Bits of broken knowledge brittle and dead,
Whether it would not be better
To hide one's head in the warm sand of sleep
And be embalmed without hustle or bother.

The rooks bicker heckle bargain always
And market carts lumber –
Let me in the calm of the all-humouring sun
Also indulge my humour
And bury myself beyond creaks and cawings
In a below world, a bottom world of amber.

Louis MacNeice

JUNE

Yes. I remember Adlestrop –
The name, because one afternoon
Of heat the express-train drew up there
Unwontedly. It was late June.

The steam hissed. Someone cleared his throat.
No one left and no one came
On the bare platform. What I saw
Was Adlestrop – only the name

And willows, willow-herb, and grass,
And meadowsweet, and haycocks dry,
No whit less still and lonely fair
Than the high cloudlets in the sky.

And for that minute a blackbird sang
Close by, and round him, mistier,
Farther and farther, all the birds
Of Oxfordshire and Gloucestershire.

Edward Thomas

So many birds have come along,
The nightingale brings her sweet song,
With lease to charm, by her own self,
The nights of this best month in twelve.
To sit up all a night in June
With that sweet bird and a full moon –
The moon with all Heav'n for her worth,
The nightingale to have this earth,
And there we are for joy – we three.
And here's the swallow, wild and free,
Prince flyer of the air by day;
For doth he not, in human way,
Dive, float and use side strokes, like men
Swimming in some clear lake? And then,
See how he skates the iceless pond!
And lo! the lark springs from the land;
He sees a ladder to Heaven's gate,
And, step by step, without abate,
He mounts it singing, back and forth;
Till twenty steps or more from earth,
On his return, then without sound
He jumps, and stone-like drops to ground.
And here are butterflies; poor things
Amazed with new-created wings;
They in the air-waves roll distrest
Like ships at sea; and when they rest
They cannot help but ope and close
Their wings, like babies with their toes.

W H Davies

Up this green woodland-ride let's softly rove,
And list the nightingale – she dwells just here.
Hush! let the wood-gate softly clap, for fear
The noise might drive her from her home of love;
For here I've heard her many a merry year –
At morn, at eve, nay, all the livelong day,
As though she lived on song. This very spot,
Just where that old man's beard all wildly trails
Rude arbours o'er the road and stops the way –
And where that child its bluebell flowers hath got,
Laughing and creeping through the mossy rails –
There have I hunted like a very boy,
Creeping on hands and knees through matted thorn
To find her nest and see her feed her young.
And vainly did I many hours employ:
All seemed as hidden as a thought unborn.
And where those crimping fern-leaves ramp among
The hazel's under-boughs, I've nestled down
And watched her while she sung; and her renown
Hath made me marvel that so famed a bird
Should have no better dress than russet brown.
Her wings would tremble in her ecstasy,
And feathers stand on end, as 'twere with joy,
And mouth wide open to release her heart
Of its out-sobbing songs. The happiest part
Of summer's fame she shared, for so to me
Did happy fancies shapen her employ;
But if I touched a bush or scarcely stirred,
All in a moment stopt. I watched in vain:
The timid bird had left the hazel bush,
And at a distance hid to sing again.   *John Clare*

This is the weather the cuckoo likes,
        And so do I;
When showers betumble the chestnut spikes,
        And nestlings fly:
And the little brown nightingale bills his best,
And they sit outside at 'The Traveller's Rest',
And maids come forth sprig-muslin drest,
And citizens dream of the south and west,
        And so do I.

This is the weather the shepherd shuns,
    And so do I;
When beeches drip in browns and duns,
    And thresh, and ply;
And hill-hid tides throb, throe on throe,
And meadow rivulets overflow,
And drops on gate-bars hang in a row,
And rooks in families homeward go,
    And so do I.   *Thomas Hardy*

Yes, it was the mountain Echo,
Solitary, clear, profound,
Answering to the shouting Cuckoo,
Giving to her sound for sound!

Unsolicited reply
To a babbling wanderer sent;
Like her ordinary cry,
Like – but oh, how different!

Hears not also mortal Life?
Hear not we, unthinking Creatures!
Slaves of folly, love, or strife –
Voices of two different natures?

Have not *we* too? – yes, we have
Answers, and we know not whence;
Echoes from beyond the grave,
Recognised intelligence!

Such rebounds our inward ear
Catches sometimes from afar –
Listen, ponder, hold them dear;
For of God, – of God they are.
    William Wordsworth

Ye airs of sunny spring that softly blow
With whisp'ry breathings o'er the grasses' blade,
Ye grass-bespangling flow'rs – too soon to fade –
That now in gemlike brightness round me grow:
Ye saplings, and ye greenbough'd trees, that throw
Your waving shadows on the sunny glade;
Thou lowland stream, whose winding waters flow,
Like molten silver, to the hoarse cascade:

Give vice the noisy town; and let the great
Ride mighty o'er the earth with pride and pow'r,
Give avarice his gold; but let me flee

Where cold and selfish hearts live not to hate
And scorn. Oh take me to thy lonely bow'r,
Sweet rural nature! Life is dear for thee.

William Barnes

As I listened from a beach-chair in the shade
To all the noises that my garden made,
It seemed to me only proper that words
Should be withheld from vegetables and birds.

A robin with no Christian name ran through
The Robin-Anthem which was all it knew,
And rustling flowers for some third party waited
To say which pairs, if any, should get mated.

No one of them was capable of lying,
There was not one which knew that it was dying
Or could have with a rhythm or a rhyme
Assumed responsibility for time.

Let them leave language to their lonely betters
Who count some days and long for certain letters;
We, too, make noises when we laugh or weep,
Words are for those with promises to keep.

W H Auden

34

JULY

From brightening fields of ether fair-disclosed,
Child of the sun, refulgent Summer comes,
In pride of youth, and felt through nature's depth:
He comes attended by the sultry hours
And ever-fanning breezes, on his way;
While, from his ardent look, the turning Spring
Averts her blushing face; and earth and skies,
All-smiling, to his hot dominion leaves.

Hence, let me haste into the mid-wood shade,
Where scarce a sunbeam wanders through
        the gloom;
And, on the dark-green grass, beside the brink
Of haunted stream, that by the roots of oak
Rolls o'er the rocky channel, lie at large,
And sing the glories of the circling year.

James Thomson

Now swarthy summer, by rude health embrowned,
  Precedence takes of rosy-fingered spring;
And laughing joy, with wild flowers pranked and
      crowned,
    A wild and giddy thing,
And health robust, from every care unbound,
    Come on the zephyr's wing,
        And cheer the toiling clown.

Me not the noise of brawling pleasure cheers,
    In nightly revels or in city streets,
But joys which soothe, and not distract the ears,
    That one at leisure meets
In the green woods, and meadows summer-shorn,
    Or fields, where bee-fly greets
        The ears with mellow horn.

The green-swathed grasshopper on treble pipe
    Sings there, and dances in mad-hearted pranks;
There bees go courting every flower that's ripe,
    On baulks and sunny banks;
And droning dragon-fly on rude bassoon
    Attempts to give God thanks
        In no discordant tune . . .

I love at early morn, from new-mown swath,
    To see the startled frog his route pursue,
And mark while, leaping o'er the dripping path,
    His bright sides scatter dew;
And early lark that from its bustle flies
    To hail his matin new;
        And watch him to the skies:

And note on hedgerow baulks, in moisture sprent,
    The jetty snail creep from the mossy thorn,
With earnest heed and tremulous intent,
    Frail brother of the morn,
That from the tiny bents and misted leaves
    Withdraws his timid horn,
        And fearful vision weaves . . .

Rich music breathes in summer's every sound;
    And in her harmony of varied greens,
Woods, meadows, hedgerows, cornfields,
        all around
    Much beauty intervenes,
Filling with harmony the ear and eye;
    While o'er the mingling scenes
            Far spreads the laughing sky.   *John Clare*

The butterfly, a cabbage-white,
(His honest idiocy of flight)
Will never now, it is too late,
Master the art of flying straight,
Yet has – who knows so well as I? –
A just sense of how not to fly:
He lurches here and here by guess
And God and hope and hopelesness.
Even the aerobatic swift
Has not his flying-crooked gift.   *Robert Graves*

A baby watched a ford. whereto
        A wagtail came for drinking;
A blaring bull went wading through,
        The wagtail showed no shrinking.

A stallion splashed his way across,
        The birdie nearly sinking;
He gave his plumes a twitch and toss,
        And held his own unblinking.

Next saw the baby round the spot
        A mongrel slowly slinking;
The wagtail gazed, but faltered not
        In dip and sip and prinking.

A perfect gentleman then neared;
        The wagtail, in a winking,
With terror rose and disappeared;
        The baby fell a-thinking.   *Thomas Hardy*

Her sight is short, she comes quite near;
A foot to me's a mile to her;
And she is known as Jenny Wren,
The smallest bird in England. When
I heard that little bird at first,
Methought her frame would surely burst
With earnest song. Oft had I seen
Her running under leaves so green,
Or in the grass when fresh and wet,
As though her wings she would forget.
And, seeing this, I said to her –
'My pretty runner, you prefer
To be a thing to run unheard
Through leaves and grass, and not a bird!'
'Twas then she burst, to prove me wrong,
Into a sudden storm of song;
So very loud and earnest, I
Feared she would break her heart and die.
'Nay, nay,' I laughed, 'be you no thing
To run unheard, sweet scold, but sing!
O I could hear your voice near me,
Above the din in that oak tree,
When almost all the twigs on top
Had starlings singing without stop.'

W H Davies

As there, along the elmy hedge, I go
  By banksides white with parsley – parsley-bloom –
Where smell of new-mown hay comes wafted by
  On wind of dewy evening, evening gloom,
And homeward take my shaded way between
The hedge's high-tipp'd wood, and barley green,
    I sing, or mean
'O troubles of the day. Flee to the west,
Come not my homeward way. I seek my rest.'

The dairy cows, by meadow trees, lie free
  Of calls to milkers' pails – the milkmaids' calls;
The horses now have left their rolling wheels
  And reel'd in home to stable, to their stalls,
And down the grey-pool'd stream the fish awhile
Are free from all the prowling angler's guile,
    And o'er the stile
I sink, and sing or say, 'Flee to the west
O troubles of the day. I seek my rest.'

My boy – whose little high-rigged boat, athwart
  The windy pool, by day, at afternoon,
Has fluttered, tippling like a bird
  That tries to fly unfledged, to fly too soon –
Now sleeps forgetful of the boat, and fond
Old dog that he had taught to swim the pond.
    So flee beyond
The edge of sinking day, towards the west,
Ye troubles flee away. I seek my rest.

A star is o'er the tower on the hill,
  Whence rings no clanging knell, no evening peal;
The mill stands dark beside the flouncing foam;
  But still is all its gear, its mossy wheel.
No rooks now sweep along the darkened sky,
And o'er the road few feet or wheels go by.
    So fly, O fly
Ye troubles, with the day, adown the west,
Come not along my way. I seek my rest.

William Barnes

AUGUST

There's something rich and joyful to the mind
To view through close and field those crooked shreds
Of footpaths that most picturesquely wind
From town to town, or some tree-hidden sheds
Where lonely cottager life's peace enjoys,
Far, far from strife and all its troubled noise;
The pent-up artisan, by pleasure led
Along their winding ways, right glad employs
His sabbath leisure in the freshening air;
The grass, the trees, the sunny sloping sky,
From his week's prison gives delicious fare;
But still he passes almost vacant by
The many charms that poesy finds to please
Along the little footpaths such as these.

Now tracking fields where passenger appears
As wading to his waist in crowding grain,
Wherever as we pass the bending ears
Pat at our sides and gain their place again;
Then crooked stile, with little steps that aid
The climbing, meets us; and the pleasant grass
And hedgerows old with arbours ready made
For weariness to rest in pleasant shade
Surround us; and with ecstasy we pass
Wild flower and insect tribes that ever mate
With joy and dance from every step we take
In numberless confusion; all employ
Their little aims for peace and pleasure's sake,
And every summer's footpath leads to joy.

John Clare

Lord, when I look at lovely things which pass,
    Under old trees the shadows of young leaves
Dancing to please the wind along the grass,
    Or the gold stillness of the August sun on the
            August sheaves;
Can I believe there is a heavenlier world than this?
    And if there is
Will the strange heart of any everlasting thing
    Bring me these dreams that take my breath away?
They come at evening with the home-flying rooks
            and the scent of hay,
    Over the fields. They come in Spring.

Charlotte Mew

The shades may show the time of day,
And flowers how summer wanes away.

Where thyme on turfy banks may grow,
Or mallows by the laneside ledge,
About the blue-barr'd gate, may show
Their grey-blue heads beside the hedge,

Or where the poppy's scarlet crown
May nod by clover, dusky red,
Or where the field is ruddy brown,
By brooks with shallow-water'd bed,

The shades may show the time of day,
And flowers how summer wanes away.

Or, where the light of dying day
May softly shine against the wall,
Below the sloping thatch, brown-grey,
Or over pale-green grass, may fall,
Or where, in fields that heat burns dry,
May show the thistle's purple studs,
Or beds of dandelions ply
Their stems with yellow fringed buds,

There shades may show the time of day,
And flowers how summer wanes away.

William Barnes

O Blackbird! sing me something well:
    While all the neighbours shoot thee round,
    I keep smooth plats of fruitful ground,
Where thou may'st warble, eat and dwell.

The espaliers and the standards all
    Are thine; the range of lawn and park:
    The unnetted black-hearts ripen dark,
All thine, against the garden wall.

Yet, tho' I spared thee all the spring,
    Thy sole delight is, sitting still,
    With that gold dagger of thy bill
To fret the summer jenneting.

A golden bill! thy silver tongue,
    Cold February loved, is dry:
    Plenty corrupts the melody
That made thee famous once, when young:

And in the sultry garden-squares,
  Now thy flute-notes are changed to coarse,
  I hear thee not at all, or hoarse
As when a hawker hawks his wares.

Take warning! He that will not sing
  While yon sun prospers in the blue,
  Shall sing for want, ere leaves are new,
Caught in the frozen palms of Spring.

Lord Tennyson

The poetry of earth is never dead:
When all the birds are faint with the hot sun,
And hide in cooling trees, a voice will run
From hedge to hedge about the new-mown mead;
That is the Grasshopper's – he takes the lead
In summer luxury, – he has never done
With his delights; for when tired out with fun
He rests at ease beneath some pleasant weed.
The poetry of earth is ceasing never:
On a lone winter evening, when the frost
Has wrought a silence, from the stove there shrills
The Cricket's song, in warmth increasing ever,
And seems to one in drowsiness half lost,
The Grasshopper's among some grassy hills.

John Keats

As I went eastward, ere the sun had set,
His yellow light on bough by bough was bright.

And there, by buttercups beside the hill,
Below the elmtrees, cow by cow was bright.

While after hairy-headed horses' heels,
With slowly-rolling wheels, the plough was bright.

And up among the people, on the sides,
One lovely face, with sunny brow, was bright.

And aye, for that one face, the bough, and cow,
And plough, in my sweet fancy, now are bright.

William Barnes

The flame-red moon, the harvest moon,
Rolls along the hills, gently bouncing,
A vast balloon,
Till it takes off, and sinks upward
To lie in the bottom of the sky, like a gold doubloon

The harvest moon has come,
Booming softly through heaven, like a bassoon.
And earth replies all night, like a deep drum.

So people can't sleep,
So they go out where elms and oak trees keep
A kneeling vigil, in a religious hush.
The harvest moon has come!

And all the moonlit cows and all the sheep
Stare up at her petrified, while she swells
Filling heaven, as if red hot, and sailing
Closer and closer like the end of the world

Till the gold fields of stiff wheat
Cry 'We are ripe, reap us!' and the rivers
Sweat from the melting hills.

Ted Hughes

SEPTEMBER

Look, stranger, at this island now
The leaping light for your delight discovers,
Stand stable here
And silent be,
That through the channels of the ear
May wander like a river
The swaying sound of the sea.

Here at the small field's ending pause
Where the chalk wall falls to the foam,
and its tall ledges
Oppose the pluck
And knock of the tide,
And the shingle scrambles after the suck-
ing surf, and the gull lodges
A moment on its sheer side.

45

Far off like floating seeds the ships
Diverge on urgent voluntary errands;
And the full view
Indeed may enter
And move in memory as now these clouds do,
That pass in the harbour mirror
And all the summer through the water saunter.

W H Auden

I see at last our great Lamorna Cove,
Which, danced on by ten thousand silver feet,
Has all those waves that run like little lambs,
To draw the milk from many a rocky teat,
Spilt in white gallons all along the shore.
Who ever saw more beauty under the sun?
I look and look, and say, 'No wonder here's
A light I never saw on earth before –
Two heavens are shining here instead of one.'
And, like the white gulls flashing in my sight,
Each furious thought that's driving through my
    brain
Screams in its fresh young wonder and delight.

W H Davies

The swallow of summer, she toils all summer,
A blue-dark knot of glittering voltage,
A whiplash swimmer, a fish of the air.
    But the serpent of cars that crawls
    through the dust
    In shimmering exhaust
    Searching to slake
    Its fever in ocean
    Will play and be idle or else it will bust.

The swallow of summer, the barbed harpoon,
She flings from the furnace, a rainbow of purples,
Dips her glow in the pond and is perfect.

But the serpent of cars that collapsed
at the beach
A scamper of colours
Which roll like tomatoes
Nude as tomatoes
With sand in their creases
To cringe in the sparkle of rollers and screech.

The swallow of summer, the seamstress of summer
She scissors the blue into shapes and she sews it,
She draws a long thread and she knots it at corners.
But the holiday people
Are laid out like wounded
Flat as in ovens
Roasting and basting
With faces of torment as space burns them blue
Their heads are transistors
Their teeth grit on sand grains
Their lost kids are squalling
While man-eating flies
Jab electric shock needles but what can they do?

They can climb in their cars with raw bodies,
raw faces
And start up the serpent
And headache it homeward
A car full of squabbles
And sobbing and stickiness
With sand in their crannies
Inhaling petroleum
That pours from the foxgloves
While the evening swallow
The swallow of summer, cartwheeling
through crimson,
Touches the honey-slow river and turning
Returns to the hand stretched from under the eaves –
A boomerang of rejoicing shadow.   *Ted Hughes*

I sat me where an ash tree's head
   From o'er a bankside reach'd around,
With outcast shade that overspread
   Some grass, and eke some stubbled ground,
While hedges up the hillock's brows
Held out their now befruited boughs.

There near the wheatrick's yellow back,
   That shone like gold before the sky,
Some rooks with wings of glossy black
   Came on down wheeling from on high,
And lightly pitched upon their feet
Among the stubble of the wheat.

And then some swallows floated by,
   All sweeping out their airy bow,
And rising up from low to high,
   Or sweeping down from high to low,
Now soon to strike their longer flight,
Away from our land's chilly light.

'The rooks', I thought, 'will still behold,
   These trees, leafbare, in driven sleet,
The swallows shun our winter cold
   For clearer skies and glowing heat.
And which is best? To have no year
Of home, or lifelong dwelling here?'

On sunny days we often yearn
   To speed us to some other land,
And men of other tongues, and learn
   Their ways of life, and works of hand;
Aye, how the world of lands is fill'd
With many menkinds many-skilled.

But since we lack the wings of gold
   That waft men over all the earth,
And find our livelihood withhold
   Our life to this our land of birth;
So let it be, since like a dove
We find us here enough to love.

                              William Barnes

Tell me not here, it needs not saying,
  What tune the enchantress plays
In aftermaths of soft September
  Or under blanching mays,
For she and I were long acquainted
  And I knew all her ways.

On russet floors, by waters idle,
  The pine lets fall its cone;
The cuckoo shouts all day at nothing
  In leafy dells alone;
And traveller's joy beguiles in autumn
  Hearts that have lost their own.

On acres of the seeded grasses
  The changing burnish heaves;
Or marshalled under moons of harvest
  Stand still all night the sheaves;
Or beeches strip in storms for winter
  And stain the wind with leaves.

Possess, as I possessed a season,
  The countries I resign,
Where over elmy plains the highway
  Would mount the hills and shine,
And full of shade the pillared forest
  Would murmur and be mine.

For nature, heartless, witless nature,
  Will neither care nor know
What stranger's feet may find the meadow
  And trespass there and go,
Nor ask amid the dews of morning
  If they are mine or no.   *A E Housman*

OCTOBER

The leaves of autumn drop by twos and threes,
And a black cloud hung o'er the old low church
Is fixed as is a rock that never stirs.
But look again and you may well perceive
The weathercock is in another sky,
And the cloud passing leaves the blue behind.

Crimson and yellow, blotched with iron-brown,
The autumn tans and variegates the leaves;
The nuts are ripe in woods about the town;
Russet the cleared fields where the bindweed weave
Round stubbles and still flowers; the trefoil seeds
And troubles all the lands. From rig to furrow
There's nothing left but rubbish and foul weeds.
I love to see the rabbits' snug-made burrow
Under the old hedge-bank or huge mossed oak
Claspt fast with ivy – there the rabbit breeds
Where the kite peelews and the ravens croak
And hares and rabbits at their leisure feed,
As varying autumn through her changes runs,
Season of sudden storms and brilliant suns.

John Cla

Cock stubble-searching pheasant, delicate
Stepper, Cathayan bird, you fire
The landscape, as across the hollow lyre
Quick fingers burn the moment: call your mate
From the deep woods tonight, for your surprised
Metallic summons answers me like wire
Thrilling with messages, and I cannot wait
To catch its evening import, half-surmised.
Others may speak these things, but you alone
Fear never noise, make the damp thickets ring
With your assertions, set the afternoon
Alight with coloured pride. Your image glows
At autumn's centre – bright, unquestioning
Exotic bird, haunter of autumn hedgerows.

Sidney Keyes

See! from the brake the whirring pheasant springs,
And mounts exulting on triumphant wings:
Short is his joy; he feels the fiery wound,
Flutters in blood, and panting beats the ground.
Ah! what avail his glossy, varying dyes,
His purple crest, and scarlet-circled eyes,
The vivid green his shining plumes unfold,
His painted wings, and breast that flames with gold?

Alexander Pope

Come, pensive Autumn, with thy clouds, and storms,
    And falling leaves, and pastures lost to flowers;
A luscious charm hangs on thy faded forms,
    More sweet than Summer in her loveliest hours,
Who, in her blooming uniform of green,
    Delights with samely and continued joy:
But give me, Autumn, where thy hand hath been,

For there is wildness that can never cloy –
The russet hue of fields left bare, and all
The tints of leaves and blossoms ere they fall.
   In thy dull days of clouds a pleasure comes,
Wild music softens in thy hollow winds;
   And in thy fading woods a beauty blooms,
That's more than dear to melancholy minds.

John Clare

To-day I think
Only with scents, – scents dead leaves yield,
And bracken, and wild carrot's seed,
And the square mustard field;

Odours that rise
When the spade wounds the root of tree,
Rose, currant, raspberry, or goutweed,
Rhubarb or celery;

The smoke's smell, too,
Flowing from where a bonfire burns
The dead, the waste, the dangerous,
And all to sweetness turns.

It is enough
To smell, to crumble the dark earth,
While the robin sings over again
Sad songs of Autumn mirth.   Edward Thomas

Now is the time for the burning of the leaves.
They go to the fire; the nostril pricks with smoke
Wandering slowly into a weeping mist.
Brittle and blotched, ragged and rotten sheaves!
A flame seizes the smouldering ruin and bites
On stubborn stalks that crackle as they resist.

The last hollyhock's fallen tower is dust;
All the spices of June are a bitter reek,
All the extravagant riches spent and mean.
All burns! The reddest rose is a ghost;
Sparks whirl up, to expire in the mist: the wild
Fingers of fire are making corruption clean.

Now is the time for stripping the spirit bare,
Time for the burning of days ended and done,
Idle solace of things that have gone before:
Rootless hopes and fruitless desire are there;
Let them go to the fire, with never a look behind
The world that was ours is a world that is ours
  no more.

They will come again, the leaf and the flower
  to arise
From squalor of rottenness into the old splendour,
And magical scents to a wondering memory bring;
The same glory, to shine upon different eyes.
Earth cares for her own ruins, naught for ours.
Nothing is certain, only the certain spring.
       Laurence Binyon

The robin whistles again. Day's arches narrow.
Tender and quiet skies lighten the withering
  flowers.
The dark of winter must come. . . . But that tiny
  arrow,
Circuiting high in the blue – the year's last
  swallow,
Knows where the coast of far mysterious sun-wild
  Africa lours.   *Walter de la Mare*

53

NOVEMBER

There's nothing like the sun as the year dies,
Kind as it can be, this world being made so,
To stones and men and beasts and birds and flies,
To all things that it touches except snow,
Whether on mountain side or street of town.
The south wall warms me: November has begun,
Yet never shone the sun as fair as now
While the sweet last-left damsons from the bough
With spangles of the morning's storm drop down
Because the starling shakes it, whistling what
Once swallows sang. But I have not forgot
That there is nothing, too, like March's sun,
Like April's, or July's, or June's, or May's,
Or January's, or February's, great days:
August, September, October, and December
Have equal days, all different from November.
No day of any month but I have said –
Or, if I could live long enough, should say –
'There's nothing like the sun that shines to-day.'
There's nothing like the sun till we are dead.

Edward Thomas

The trees are undressing, and fling in many
    places –
On the gray road, the roof, the window-sill –
Their radiant robes and ribbons and yellow laces;
A leaf each second so is flung at will,
Here, there, another and another, still and still.

A spider's web has caught one while
    downcoming,
That stays there dangling when the rest pass on;
Like a suspended criminal hangs he, mumming
In golden garb, while one yet green, high yon,
Trembles, as fearing such a fate for himself anon.

Thomas Hardy

Fall, leaves, fall; die, flowers, away;
Lengthen night and shorten day,
Every leaf speaks bliss to me
Fluttering from the autumn tree.
I shall smile when wreaths of snow
Blossom where the rose should grow;
I shall sing when night's decay
Ushers in a drearier day.

Emily Brontë

I'm glad we have wood in store awhile,
For soon we must shut the door awhile,
As winterly winds may roar awhile,
    And scatter the whirling snow.

The swallows have now all hied away,
And most of the flowers have died away,
And boughs, with their leaves all dried away,
    Are windbeaten to and fro.

Your walks in the ashtree droves are cold,
Your banks in the timber'd groves are cold,
Your seats in the garden coves are cold,
    Where sunheat did lately glow.

No rosebud is blooming red to-day,
No pink for your breast or head to-day,
O'erhanging the garden bed to-day,
  Is nodding its sweet head low.

No more is the swinging lark above,
And air overclouded dark above
So baffles the sun's last spark above,
  That shadows no longer show.

So now let your warm cheek bloom to-night,
While fireflames heat the room to-night,
Dispelling the flickering gloom to-night,
  While winds of the winter blow.

William Barnes

Beech-wood fires are bright and clear
If the logs are kept a year,
Oaken logs burn steadily
If the wood is old and dry.
Chestnut's only good, they say,
If for long it's laid away.
      But ash new or ash old
      Is fit for a Queen with a crown of gold.

Birch and fir-logs burn too fast –
Blaze up bright but do not last.
Make a fire of elder-tree,
Death within your house you'll see.
It is by the Irish said
Hawthorn bakes the sweetest bread.
      But ash green or ash brown
      Is fit for a Queen with a golden crown.

Elm-wood burns like churchyard mould –
E'en the very flames are cold.
Poplar gives a bitter smoke
Fills your eyes and makes you choke.
Apple-wood will scent your room
With an incense-like perfume.
      But ash wet or ash dry
      For a Queen to warm her slippers by.

Anon

These flowers survive their lover bees,
    Whose deep bass voices filled the air;
The cuckoo and the nightingale
    Have come and gone, we know not where.

Now, in this green and silent world,
    In Autumn, full of smiling light,
I hear a bird that, suddenly,
    Startles my hearing and my sight.

It is the Robin, singing of
    A silver world of snow and frost;
Where all is cold and white – except
    The fire that's on his own warm breast.

                                        W H Davies

The robin, tamest of the feather'd race,
Soon as he hears the woodman's sounding chops,
With ruddy bosom and a simple face
Around his old companion fearless hops,
And there for hours in pleas'd attention stops:
The woodman's heart is tender and humane,
And at his meals he many a crumble drops.
Thanks to thy generous feelings, gentle swain;
And what thy pity gives, shall not be given
    in vain.

The woodman gladly views the closing day,
To see the sun drop down behind the wood,
Sinking in clouds deep blue or misty grey,
Round as a foot-ball and as red as blood:
The pleasing prospect does his heart much good,
Though 'tis not his such beauties to admire;
He hastes to fill his bags with billet-wood,
Well-pleas'd from the chill prospect to retire,
To seek his corner chair, and warm snug
    cottage fire.   *John Clare*

When Winter's ahead,
What can you read in November
That you read in April
When Winter's dead?

I hear the thrush, and I see
Him alone at the end of the lane
Near the bare poplar's tip,
Singing continuously.

Is it more that you know
Than that, even as in April,
So in November,
Winter is gone that must go?

Or is all your lore
Not to call November November,
And April April,
And Winter Winter – no more?

But I know the months all,
And their sweet names, April,
May and June and October,
As you call and call

I must remember
What died in April
And consider what will be born
Of a fair November;

And April I love for what
It was born of, and November
For what it will die in,
What they are and what they are not,

While you love what is kind,
What you can sing in
And love and forget in
All that's ahead and behind.

Edward Thomas

DECEMBER

Sweet chestnuts brown like soling leather turn;
The larch-trees, like the colour of the sun;
That paled sky in the autumn seemed to burn,
What a strange scene before us now does run –
Red, brown, and yellow, russet, black, and dun;
Whitethorn, wild cherry, and the poplar bare;
The sycamore all withered in the sun.
No leaves are now upon the birch-tree there:
All now is stript to the cold wintry air.

See, not one tree but what has lost its leaves –
And yet the landscape wears a pleasing hue.
The winter chill on his cold bed receives
Foliage which once hung o'er the waters blue.
Naked and bare the leafless trees repose.
Blue-headed titmouse now seeks maggots rare,
Sluggish and dull the leaf-strewn river flows;
That is not green, which was so through the year
Dark chill November draweth to a close.

'Tis winter, and I love to read indoors,
When the moon hangs her crescent up on high;
While on the window shutters the wind roars,

And storms like furies pass remorseless by.
How pleasant on a feather-bed to lie,
Or, sitting by the fire, in fancy soar
With Dante or with Milton to regions high,
Or read fresh volumes we've not seen before,
Or o'er old Burton's *Melancholy* pore.   *John Clare*

December stillness, teach me through your trees
That loom along the west, one with the land,
The veiled evangel of your mysteries.
    While nightfall, sad and spacious, on the down
    Deepens, and dusk imbues me, where I stand,
    With grave diminishings of green and brown,
    Speak, roofless Nature, your instinctive words;
    And let me learn your secret from the sky,
    Following a flock of steadfast-journeying birds
    In lone remote migration beating by.
December stillness, crossed by twilight roads,
Teach me to travel far and bear my loads.

Siegfried Sassoon

In a drear-nighted December,
    Too happy, happy tree,
Thy branches ne'er remember
    Their green felicity:
    The north cannot undo them,
    With a sleety whistle through them;
    Nor frozen thawings glue them
        From budding at the prime.

In a drear-nighted December,
    Too happy, happy brook,
Thy bubblings ne'er remember
    Apollo's summer look;
    But with a sweet forgetting,
    They stay their crystal fretting,
    Never, never petting
        About the frozen time.

Ah! would 'twere so with many
    A gentle girl and boy!
But were there ever any
    Writh'd not at passed joy?
  To know the change and feel it,
  When there is none to heal it,
  Nor numbed sense to steal it,
      Was never said in rhyme.   *John Keats*

The warm sun is failing, the bleak wind
     is wailing,
The bare boughs are sighing, the pale flowers
     are dying
        And the Year
On the earth her death-bed, in a shroud
     of leaves dead,
        Is lying.
    Come, Months, come away,
    From November to May,
    In your saddest array;
    Follow the bier
    Of the dead cold Year,
And like dim shadows watch by her sepulchre.

The chill rain is falling, the nipped worm
     is crawling,
The rivers are swelling, the thunder is knelling
       For the Year;
The blithe swallows are flown, and the lizards
     each gone
        To his dwelling.
    Come, Months, come away;
    Put on white, black, and grey;
    Let your light sisters play –
    Ye, follow the bier
    Of the dead cold Year,
And make her grave green with tear on tear.
               Percy Bysshe Shelley

Is it not fine to walk in spring,
When leaves are born, and hear birds sing?
And when they lose their singing powers,
In summer, watch the bees at flowers?
Is it not fine, when summer's past,
To have the leaves, no longer fast,
Biting my heel where'er I go,
Or dancing lightly on my toe?
Now winter's here and rivers freeze;
As I walk out I see the trees,
Wherein the pretty squirrels sleep,
All standing in the snow so deep:
And every twig, however small,
Is blossomed white and beautiful.
Then welcome, winter, with thy power
To make this tree a big white flower;
To make this tree a lovely sight,
With fifty brown arms draped in white,
While thousands of small fingers show
In soft white gloves of purest snow.

W H Davies

I watch a dung-cart stumble by
    Leading the harvest to the fields,
That from cow-byre and stall and sty
    The farmstead in the winter yields.

Like shocks in a reaped field of rye
    The small black heaps of lively dung
Sprinkled in the grass-meadow lie
    Licking the air with smoky tongue.

This is Earth's food that man piles up
    And with his fork will thrust on her,
And Earth will lie and slowly sup
    With her moist mouth through half the year.

Andrew Young

The frost is here,
And fuel is dear,
And woods are sear,
And fires burn clear,
And frost is here
And has bitten the heel of the going year.

Bite, frost, bite!
You roll up away from the light
The blue wood-louse, and the plump dormouse,
And the bees are still'd, and the flies are kill'd,
And you bite far into the heart of the house,
But not into mine.

Bite, frost, bite!
The woods are all the searer,
The fuel is all the dearer,
The fires are all the clearer,
My spring is all the nearer,
You have bitten into the heart of the earth,
But not into mine.   *Lord Tennyson*

Good husband and housewife now chiefly be glad
Things handsome to have as they ought to be had,
They both do provide against Christmas to come,
To welcome good neighbour, good cheer
        to have some.
Good bread and good drink, a good fire
        in the hall,
Brawn, pudding and souse, and good mustard
        withall.
Beef, mutton and porke, shred pies of the best.
Pig, veal, goose and capon and turkey
        well dressed.
Cheese, apples and nuts, jolly carols to hear,
As then in the country is counted good cheer.

What cost to good husband is any of this?
Good household provision only it is.
Of other the like I do leave out a many.
It costeth the husbandman never a penny.

                    Thomas Tusser

ACKNOWLEDGEMENTS

Permission to use copyright material is gratefully
acknowledged to the following:

POEMS: Mrs Nicolete Gray and The Society of Authors on
behalf of the Laurence Binyon Estate (extract from a poem by
Laurence Binyon); Oxford University Press and the author
(*Collected Poems* by Basil Bunting); the executors of the W H
Davies estate and Jonathan Cape (*The Complete Poems of W H
Davies*); the literary trustees of Walter de la Mare and The
Society of Authors as their representative (*Inward Com-
panions* by Walter de la Mare); Faber & Faber (*Season Songs* by
Ted Hughes, *Collected Poems* by W H Auden, *The Collected
Poems of Louis MacNeice*); Robert Graves (*Collected Poems*); The
Society of Authors as literary representatives of the estate of
A E Housman, and Jonathan Cape (*Collected Poems* by A E
Housman); Routledge & Kegan Paul (*Collected Poems* by
Sidney Keyes); Gerald Duckworth (*Collected Poems* by
Charlotte Mew); Poetry Nottingham Publications and the
author (*A Birch Tree with Finches* by Betty Parvin); George
Sassoon (*Collected Poems* by Siegfried Sassoon); Mrs
Myfanwy Thomas and Faber & Faber (*Collected Poems* by
Edward Thomas); the literary estate of Virginia Woolf
(*Another World Than This* by Vita Sackville-West); Martin
Secker & Warburg, the author and Leonard Clark, editor
(*Complete Poems* by Andrew Young).

WOOD ENGRAVINGS (figures in brackets refer to page
numbers in *Rural Rhymes*): The Hon Lady Betjeman (letter
heading design, 26); Mrs John Carter (colophon for Halcyon-
Commonwealth Foundation, 36); Faber & Faber (*The Open
Air* by Adrian Bell, 12, 17, 22, 25; *Tribute to Benjamin Britten on
his Fiftieth Birthday*, edited by Anthony Gishford, 21, 35); J F
Grace (Cornwall Nursing Association calendar, 8, 46);
Granada Publishing (*The Skylark and Other Poems* by Ralph
Hodgson, 30, 31; Hart-Davies McGibbon colophon, 51);
Victor Gollancz Ltd (*From Darkness to Light* by Victor
Gollancz, 25); Gregynog Press (*The Praise and Happinesse of
the Countrie-Life*, 4, 64); High House Press (*Old English Wines
and Cordials*, 41); Dame Alix Meynell on behalf of Nonesuch
Press (*Confessions* by Jean-Jacques Rousseau, 60); Oxford
University Press (*Periodical* 1959, 11; *Poems, Centuries and
Three Thanksgivings*, 40); Mrs Janet Stone (16, 54, 59); Warren
Editions (*The Old Rectory*, 7, 45, 50).